looking up the down spout

poems by
Christina Quinn

©2018/2019 Christina Quinn

book design and layout: SpiNDec, Port Saint Lucie, FL
cover image: *Blue Dog* by Christina Quinn

All rights reserved.

No part of this book may be used or reproduced in any manner whatsoever without written permission except in the case of brief quotations embodied in critical articles and reviews. Members of educational institutions and organizations wishing to photocopy any of the work for classroom use, or authors, artists and publishers who would like to obtain permission for any material in the work, should contact the publisher.

Printed in the United States of America.

Published by Poetic Justice Books
Port Saint Lucie, Florida
www.poeticjusticebooks.com

ISBN: 978-1-950433-087

table of contents

i have been dying 3
he smiles lazily 4
imitation blue delft 5
in blue clear sulfur flare 6
no i never saw a nose quite like that 7
awake the ghost of you remains 8
hey beautiful, x's and o's 9
the smell of insanity 10
"c" he says 11
visiting hours 14
ever since we met 15
in the madness of life 16
from the last step sometimes 17
the hail started 18
i'm glad to see 19
i have a bear in my pocket 20
i cut hair 21
purple jersey tea in moonlight 22
under the pier 23
aren't we the perfect pair 24
behind the cover of convex lens 25
here we are 26

looking
up
the
down
spout

I have been dying
I feel no pain I dream in color
I hear sharps & flats
& speak chameleon
listen I won't lie
I have been a polite spectral guest
mostly
though not in person
see here
I know the secrets of
deathly impermanence
I don't lie

he smiles lazily
you know your problem
you feel unloved &
there ain't no flowers in the grave
in that moment when you let go of the power
i see you are not the angel behind the words
they are wholly mine in perfect synch with the day
& the hour & the time
it's a complexity of everything
thinking has become a dangerous vanity
a search, an answer untold
a mind blown darkness
& the irrational scenario
of scorched earth
you see he doesn't just do
he loves & that about says it all
under the nimbus of sainthood
i have flowers i say
while i sleep with eyes open
it's the complexity of everything
& can i ask
are we fixing to have some trouble here
don't answer

imitation blue delft
wallpapered across the chimney breast
it struck me as funny
all those repetitive windmills
unable to wave away
the odorous fancy feast prime beef cat fart
laid silently & satisfactorily
by one very smug orange cat
my mother was not amused
she'd paid good money
to a glass eyed paper hanger
his signature crooked lines not helping the intensity
   of tile
((his left eye still rolling around somewhere
   in france))
& now this
i pointed out the temporary nature of one
the permanence of the other
scheisse she said under her breath
exactly I said

in blue clear sulfur flare
under the bridge of beaked nose
& clear grey eyes
i envy the unfiltered cool
welded to the corner of your mouth
& the mystic haze of goddamned enigmas
making like truth waiting in the wings
is it a practiced love affair
like the cover of photoplay
dragged kicking & screaming
to the pretensions of #2 parkside road
a bit of class
a bit of bloody sunday best
like the best scotch no rocks
like the single breasted cut of your jib
all the girls swoon
the ladies lick lips
the men are furtive in their jealousy
& i believed in immortality
until you were gone

no i never saw a nose quite like that
it spoke of early debauchery
gluttony
lascivious intemperance
proud it was
like a schoolboy's honest erection
i fixated on the crotch of his eyebrows
eyes flicking down to the protuberance beneath
i wanted so badly to stare
at the audacity of his snout
he raised a well manicured finger
setting the left nostril a quiver with one solid tap
listen he said
my brother's is twice as big
but it's the quality that counts

awake the ghost of you remains
impeccable & smug
i'd like to kiss the grin off your face
slip serrated edges between your last rib
& the space where eve's borrowed cartilage
left a festering wound
like lancing the infection
& in that bucolic moment when apples were apples
here am i
millenniums later
paying for the disease of loving you
still wanting to belong
close to your christmas heart

hey beautiful, x's and o's
considering the situation
life's punches
the relocation of me to here
you to there
& the inevitable march of time
your message
stopped my day
a traffic jam of memories
like some rude bastard horn leaning
getting nowhere
still
the x's and o's wove an intricate path
skipping lanes
crossing double yellows
right through my heart

the smell of insanity
& track of quick eyes
silver bells of madness
disturb the air
this autopsy must end
stop seeing the body
focus on the question

are you mad she asked

with a clay heart
he replied
yes

"c" he says
there are people here
transported they are
the guy downstairs
he has wifi
& a machine that can make
anything
there's mebbe fifty
in my room
& they've populated the tree
with children
bouquets of twins
smiling at me
there's no room in here
i'm homeless
& the parents are ...
they're wearing my clothes

in the background
i hear voices
it's the tv
the dad thinks i'm mad
i'm not am i

no i say
not yet

"c" he whispers
i've seen the worst of them
retired people rabid
& doggy style
it's a brothel in here
& children are playing

in the bones of
their dead parents

oh shit oh damn
a thousand cats just
slid through the vent
i can't watch them
they're everywhere
& the dad won't help me
he watches tv all fucking day & night

"c" he says i haven't slept
it's been three days
not a five minutes free
the dad keeps taking my mental
i've bullied about five blokes &
the dad keeps watching the same movie
over & over
he can't believe
i've lost my mind
this woman
keeps throwing her hands up every time she cums
eight hundred orgasms
& the old couple are still at it
cos he's gonna die tomorrow

i'm scared "c"
i think
i've gone mad

s'ok i say
you wouldn't know
if you were really mad

thanks
he says
can you do something about these goddamn cats?
it's a brothel in here

visiting hours
actually just one
in which i must show
who & what i am
therefore i shall go in the guise of mother not lover
having been mistaken for & winked at as such in that
    stereotypical way
& so slipping incognito through the cracks
i shall perch on the edge of my chair
rigid wooden & high backed
pat hands
stroke knees
lean in to kiss
in that motherly way
& i shall whisper
28 days baby
raise one eyebrow &
the hem of my skirt
& you will know
exactly

ever since we met
retelling past histories
lives & loves
really
a staggering tonnage of shit
& waiting
waiting for verdicts
hail marys & absolutions
anyway
it's all theater
heroes & villains
demons & angels
players finding their mark
i'm gonna stop you here
we made our choices
most of them breathtakingly
unoriginal

if you've never seen the desert
let me paint you a picture
empty heat
cold nights
& sinning like love
under the stars

in the madness of life
i once saw a whale
closer than i thought
near enough to touch
his skin covered in scars
& suckered shells
but fear & the white of his eye
held me back
drove him away
a gargantuan shadow
slipping away
under crisp clean green

from the last step sometimes
i sit & feed my friends the pigeons
they understand this perpetual motion of the mind
the four cents in my pocket
& the shoe shocked horses
bolting down cobbled streets
there's a whirling field of energy
an obsessive compulsion to capture
something tantalizing & out of reach
i feel my dreams have been stolen
others have made silk from my visions
even so
i was born at the stroke of midnight
the cusp of yesterday tomorrow & today
i can tie three knots in an eyelash
i can make sparks fly
i feed my friends the crumbs of my thoughts
i jangle the cents in my pocket
i watch the horses bolt
& from my frozen finger tips
i touch the stolen dream & execute the lie

the hail started
sugar cane fronds hunkered down
beneath skies the blue black of gun metal
clouds with that sickly yellow rim
parked ominously overhead

this is exactly why we stock up
on rum & tinned peaches he said

water leaks through the ceiling
down the fragile stem holding flowered fan blades
down to the aluminum saucepan
plinking off key ragtime tunes
outside a blue fiberglass pool
skitters down tin can boulevard
he sits cross legged on the bed
opening a can with a tool from his swiss army
on the floor two jelly jars
each containing an inch of rum

see he says
when the cyclone hits ya eat a peach
swallow the rum & kiss yer ass good bye
shouldn't we evacuate i ask

nah he says forking a peach
& handing me a glass
it's too late now

i'm glad to see
you still have both earrings firmly anchored
the same pitted olive eyes behind those damned
   taped up ray bans
i see the new addition of superglue haze distorting
   fish bowl lenses
but your eyes
seemingly unaffected
wander from plate to water glass to table to me
just the same as always
today no mustache no gravelly cheek
just the goatee that comes & goes
& perhaps is another prisoner of your fancy
i watch white teeth behind full lips that speak of
   sealing wax & kings
& it's a comfort from this side of the table
behind the safety of crispy noodles
red stoppered soy sauce &
two dipping sauces
the second appletini helps too
it's a comfort to watch the hand with the basquiat
crown
adjust the slide of glasses
the rise & fall of your chest under the same
   checkered shirt
the familiarities
the gestures
the dodge of words & sentences from one topic to
   the next
like a fruit fly wandering through an over ripe
   bowl of cherries
it all makes perfect sense
oh & did i mention the hat

i have a bear in my pocket
he's not only a dancing bear no sir
he boxes
he bops
he rises tall on legs of goliath proportion
he roars
yes sir he roars like a train
& when he has your attention
he places one well honed claw in the deep waxy
   recess of your ear
reams out the mutter & clutter
gives you a shake & a bop on the cheek for good
   measure
& then we dance
yes sir
me & the bear we dance in the dust
trampling over the sign that says quite plain
do not step on the grass &
do not
do not dance on wednesdays
then we hightail it down the lane
yes sir
me n my dancing bear

i cut hair
shag
bowl
buzz
sometimes i snip ears
& shape bald patches
like maps of australia
geologic
necks become fleshy
& red like the buttocks of urine soaked babies
curls of damp
feather the floor
& surrender to birds mating & making
stray wisps become fodder for
a million cockroaches hiding in walls
i position heads left right up down
whisk towel wrapped shoulders
then
like siegfried & roy
a flourished reveal
two each of brow & eyes
raised inquiringly
fearfully
north

purple jersey tea in moonlight

it doesn't have to be complicated
we can sit on the porch & count stars
savor the night scented jasmine
&
inside our comfortable walls will sway
melting under blue notes from charlie
some will escape into the night
making whippoorwills stop to listen
& i'll be happy for years left
while you write words that bend the heart
almost to breaking point
&
the only distraction will be from cats
lounging on my old lady knees
see it doesn't have to be complicated

under the pier
sun fingers
hold tight to
green algae
softening the split
of treated wood
pink crustaceans
kiss randomly
the junctions
of dark & light
& the sea makes
entanglement
of underworld weeds
slumber eyes
catch shaded
dappled skin
swaying in time
to the tide
he smiles
in that lazy way
& the sea tilts
close enough
to taste salty skin
your eyes are green
he said

aren't we the perfect pair
halo's hanging like nooses round necks
& what started as a blaze of glory
sputtered as starved flames
a faint haze of wick wax dreams scenting the air
it's cold here without you
i dream of bougainvillea nights
seersucker days
your perfect lower lip
& the bead of salted lemon lime waiting to be licked
i should have
except for the bouncing of a ball point against your mouth
held with rock star ease
like a drummer
like a writer
about to explode words on a page
& that damned pork pie hat casting purple shades
i wanted to
i should have
but tito puente kept playing
five beat mambo

behind the cover of convex lens
the charismatic sparkle
a prism
through sun glinted windshields
one eye slightly larger
& swiveling left
it's my favorite one by the way
i like to watch as it wanders through realms
of imagination & regurgitated loves
several starring roles
& sometimes
perhaps
held captive for a moment or two
as history repeats itself
the other one
the second eye
remains fixated
briefly really
on certain cracks within the room
until jerked into new chasms of voided space
all the while
pondering perhaps
the whys of verbal lassitude
on the part of the heroine sitting opposite
chin on hand
little does he know
i am off somewhere with eye number one
a magical mystery tour
culminating in the distraction of full lips spilling words &
the vacuum between here & then & now
oh the gravity of it all
the fall from grace

here we are
bleeding cold as if
the deaths of winter
hold us captive
in strange hibernation
dreamless & alone

turn me over and start again

turn me over and start again

jefferson
*

it was the exact shade of
mustard yellow
the cut of clothe over broad
made rush of recognition
& all the years slid
softening the hard of living
that shirt
my favorite color
& the way you looked
like movies & dreams
etched gentle into
childhood memories
a faint linger of pipe
& old spice
that's all it took
& here i am
walking down jefferson
with out you

home
*

my sister & i shared a bedroom
& a window that looked over the street
lads would whistle
& that sash window would fly up
we'd hang there like two
dark haired rapunzels
carrying on &
smoking mum's cigarettes

my dad would bang on the ceiling
but he never came in
'cept that one time when
we set the toilet seat on fire
we couldn't sit down for a week after that
but mum got the last laugh
she been wanting a new toilet
for a while

we'd sit on our suitcases watching
the curve of tracks
until our train appeared
hissing & belching clouds of steam
as it shimmied to a stop

fearful breath was held as we
stepped over the yawning gap
between platform & train
we were aboard
squeezing down corridors
searching for
the perfect compartment
dad would slide open the door
hoist the bags overhead &
mum would whip out crayons & paper
a flask of tea & the inevitable
squashed sandwiches

the final whistle sounded &
the conductor swung on board
the train heaving & lurching then
settling into a soothing rhythm
through the window we saw
soot blackened buildings
passing fast
replaced by cows in meadows
& if you angled your head just right
way off in the distance
a tiny speck of bright blue sky & sea
waiting just for us

summer holidays
*

every august
rain or shine
we went on summer holidays
as the day approached
my sister and i would pack
small cardboard suitcases
the key attached to the handle by a long string
in went our bathing suits, shorts
sandals, books
& other essential things

we always took a taxi
my dad had a certain reputation
holidays were grand affairs
money was to be spent &
tut tutted over by neighbors
watching enviously from behind
lace curtains

the taxi always had a funny smell
old leather, smoke & hint of something unpleasant
still we rode in silent anticipation
noses pressed against the window
until we arrived at the train station
a soaring victorian arrangement
curlicued iron thistles
& glassed in air holding
the smell of coal fired steam
& the echo of whistles

we'd wait on the platform
under a huge clock atop an iron pillar that sprouted arms
pointing to london
bournemouth or
bridlington

it was the first time i became the trusty side kick
but not the last
we learned to tango later

dance class
*

short white socks curled over at the ankle
new red leather shoes & dresses with sashes
perfectly matched, she taller & older but
still identical to smaller me
i held my sister's hand tightly as
we walked past soot grimed sandstone &
terraced mill homes
we made a left on oxley lane
touching the two trees for luck
we were on our way to
learn the moves
of tango & quickstep
as if we would ever have the occasion
to dance among coal mines & mill chimneys

two silver half crowns
payment for dance lessons
weighted the pockets of our skirts
banging our knees as we walked
at the corner a gaggle of children waited
in front of the alhambra theater
its pink & blue minarets & morrocan arches
home to sheiks, cowboys & gangsters
& other exotic creatures of the silver screen
the half crowns knocked at our knees
reminding us we were destined for dance lessons

our red leather shoes propped up the seat in front
the once white socks held caramel smudges
from cracker jacked fingers
our eyes transfixed on masks & horses & dusty plains
my sister whispers an aside
hey our kid
we'll make up some steps on't way 'ome

six miles of love
*

bradford bus station
up side of the university
a fragrant oily smell
sluiced in from the square
curry n chips still wrapped
in the daily
the last bus
left at twelve thirty
so we ran in heels
mine stiletto
yours cuban
swung on board & up the steps
already reaching for lighter & smokes
claiming the back seat
in hopes of a good snog
this was our place
a double decker bus
two tone green
& six miles of love

the problem with sharing a bedroom
*

she came home from university
changed
sophisticated & slightly worldly
resulting in the demise of bowie's multi colored gaze
laid to waste
along with dylan's boyish sullen
hold on i said
those posters are mine
a withering look
& then
she tacked up a print of marx
there she said
much better
later on
i had to agree

mum
*

she bent down to release the heel of her shoe
caught midway on industrial steel stairs
men muttered
bloody hell
women just looked
keeping their opinions bottled
my mother never understood
why it was so hard to find
a female friend
my dad
delighted in the way she looked
blue velvet & red lips
solitary splashes of color
shocking the drab out of cold grim nights
the envy in make do hearts &
serviceable shoes tapping judgmental morse code beats
he stepped into her promise
she welcomed him with a kiss
& the silence
was audible

two crowns
*

in that delicious dare
that bone rattling ride
legs lifted high
hands gripping tight to the
argyle vested boy
standing tall on pedals &
leaning into the speed
we bumped down hill
cobbles bouncing us left & right
he yells ...
jump
i'm a missile
& scream as missiles do
hurtling out of control
to that spot
where there's nowhere else to go
leaving tiny chips of white &
streaked coppery blood
against the wall
my tongue explores
feeling for teeth &
finding only holes

banshees & ghosts
*

before it was a crime to burn coal
& margaret* had not yet closed the mines
when sandstone buildings dusted with soot
were testament to textile mills
& hard scrabble miners
there was a possibility on winter mornings
of fog so thick it seemed as if overnight
the factories had spewed their guts
clothing all in sound dulling gray worsted
street lamps managed only a feeble glow
it was as if god had forgotten to end the night

you would take my hand
as we stepped into the gloom
come on our kid you'd say
tha's nowt out here but fog & ghosties
then you'd run out into the gray nothing
shrieking like a banshee
i'd listen for tell tale footsteps
& try to slip into a new hiding place
but you always found me
then we'd walk the path to school
bouncing blood curdling screams
off the wall of damp
& counting street lamps as markers

*Margaret Thatcher

half pint
*

the dog always waited for him by the kitchen door
a magic portal leading
in a roundabout & inevitable way
to the tap room down at the albion
where they'd share a pint of best
& listen to doreen the landlady belt out
a few music hall favorites
& patrick playing along on the upright
((despite the war having stolen his left arm))
occasionally he'd join in a chorus or two
the dog that is
unable to resist those warbling high notes
he'd throw back his head & let rip
a series of ascending & descending howls
until doreen silenced him with one of her looks

after my dad died
the dog would walk down to the pub by himself
take the first opportune moment to slip through the doors
& settle himself in the corner
doreen always brought him a half of best
then she & patrick would turn out a song or two
come on she'd say
glancing over at the dog
give us a song then
but he never sang again
just drank his beer & watched

purple spring
*

two small girls each running a rutted path
& striding the middle ground
a man smoking a briar pipe &
a laughing woman calling
to a small white dog
running over the rise & through
the last of the oak trees
shaded damp & pungent grass lead down to a hidden glade
& there lay the treasure
thousands of bluebells nodding in the breeze
whooping & hollering we ran
sylvia & me
rolling into the purple of spring

gilding the words
*

he used to sing
until the illness took breath away
still. .. he hummed when the weather was good
seated at the kitchen table
((a cumbersome relic from past lives))
lovingly gilding the fore edge
of an assortment of books
binding spines & book boards
in soft moroccan leather

with his gilding pen
he wrote in fine copperplate
marking the spines
titles first & underneath
keats, byron, or blake
& his favorite
oscar wilde
he told me once
it's one thing to read their words
but you must honor them with ownership
then he glued his own 'ex libris'
((a fanciful piece by aubrey beardsley))
on to the fly leaf
all the while humming
jerusalem
that most english
of english hymns

home
*

the smell of elm trees
warming under watery sun
crisp damp earth
under moldering leaves
such perfumed comforts
bring wisps of memory
& for a few slim moments
i am striding long
a small white dog running ahead
down the bank to the canal where
moss covers the ancient walls with
a brilliant green blanket
shallow pools of rain fill the hollows
in foot worn steps

down on the towpath
the dog stops
looking back
waiting
& then he's gone
round the corner of memory

the smell of men
*

in my life
there was a split in time
when everything came into focus
a uniformed man standing tall in the garden
my mother smiling
laughing sweet high notes
quick hands making tender touch
i watched from behind sheets
billowing in the breeze of change
daddy's home he said
i was swooped high against
rough shoulders & chin
& oh the smell of him
pipe tobacco & old spice
i clung tight nosed against his neck
never wanting to leave this place
never wanting to return to
lavendar hugs
&
that's been the truth
of how it was & is & will be
the smell of men

got it
we were ballast
a counter to the tipping point
we careened around corners
at breakneck speed
teetering on two tires
the third hanging like a dog's leg as its taking a pee

eight o'clock & dark
we turned onto the magic mile
& there they were
the seven dwarves
bambi &
peter pan
all lit up & repeating robotic mechanical moves
even my sister was agog
both of us pressed up against the glass
catching as much illumination
as we could
andrew made a right hoping to come around for another look
but in the glory of it all
we forgot the vic-ee vers-ee

& that's how we ended up
in the back of police cruiser
driving up & down our street
at almost midnight
go on then said the copper
& nodded at the switch
we gleefully hit the button
swirling red & blue lights
illuminations

illuminations
*

it was andrew's fault
uncle andrew may he rest
the only family member
who owned a car
he wasn't really family
still we called him uncle anyway
& in auntie margaret's opinion
it wasn't a real car
dear god
it's only got three wheels
still it had seats
& it kept the rain out

packing potted meat sandwiches
& a thermos
we were on our way
blackpool
home of the tower
ballroom dancing
& an occasional liberace sighting
but it was the illuminations
we'd come for
a mile of cartoon characters
suspended & lit up like christmas
my sister copped a jaded attitude
she'd been last year
but this was my first trip
& in a car

alright you two
uncle andrew looked at us
through the rear view mirror
right corners lean left
& vic-ee vers-ee

roller skates
*

rattling over cracked sidewalk
knees clenched against the inevitable skin
left on grimed grey hardness
I gather speed like I know what I'm doing
sucked air held tight
& gripped stomache fear
inside my head I pirouette to a drum beat tango
my sister yells something over her shoulder
i slide into a perfect landing
wheels spinning tales into the air

down town rain
*

little old ladies check in at the door
drenched refugees
wading in from puddles as big as lakes
they shake their brollies with serious intent
wetting puddle soaked shoes &
support stockinged legs
that stand sturdy & akimbo
like catamarans in a summer monsoon

from the front step
my dad would yell
edith
& move threateningly toward mum
ponto would be there in a flash
his chest all puffed up
that rumble filling the air
mum would pat him
good boy, good dog
& snag him by the scruff

linda blackwell
my soon to be best friend
lived two doors down
she'd come over to play
we'd dress the dog
in old baby clothes
& wheel him round in the pram
one night over supper
linda said
me mum says you're a dark horse mr. hoyle
& if it weren't for the dog
mrs. hoyle would be black & blue
& the dog only goes down the pub
to bring you home

aye said dad
& ate his sausage & chips
mum said nothing
stuffing down the laugh
& slipping the dog a treat

---

* *"Ponto was the Lion's name ..."* from "Jim, Who Ran Away from His Nurse, and was eaten by a Lion" by Ken Nesbitt

whenever he got the chance
ponto would slip out the back door
race across elland road
to the cow paddock
he'd worm his way into
the nearest pile of steaming cow muck
then he'd come home
head high tail wagging
proud as punch

mum didn't think it was funny anymore
harold she'd say in her german accent
we must train him
& they did
he'd sit & beg & rollover
but the minute the door opened
which it did a lot from all the
delivery men bringing stuff for the shop
out he'd slip

sometimes dad
would head him off at the pass
a casual stroll over to the dew drop inn
money jangling in his pocket
& ponto would do a one eighty
beer replacing the thought of cows
dad would catch him at the bar
buy him a half of best
then come home
ponto leading the way

if that didn't work
the other ruse did

the dark horse
*

our dog judy got run over
a few months later
dad brought home
a small bundle of white
with a brown eye patch
& named him ponto
after the poem*

all our friends had dogs
with names like rex
prince, sheba & blackie

what kind a name is that then
they'd ask with a sneer

he's named after a poem
i began
my sister stepped on my foot
he's named after a lion
that ate a kid she said
& that shut em up

there were two things ponto loved
mum & cows
mum thought it was funny
she'd sit on the sofa
ponto on her lap
basking in the attention
dad would plop down
& the dog would give him that look
don't push yer luck
a low warning rumble
filling the space between
mum & dad

will donelley
*

waiting for the number 42
monday through friday
i'd watch him
stacking boxes
unloading delivery vans
in his white grocer's apron

quick feet
agile moves &
a shock of black hair
i studied his biceps under rolled sleeves
with schoolgirl eyes
& when i got to class
i'd write his name all over
the brown paper covering
trigonometry II

one friday
he turned
dropped the box of caulis
& walked right up to me
eyes like pieces of heaven
looked me up & down

you want to watch me fight
i've got a match
tonight at the working men's
i'll pick you up here

& that's how
i came to love boxing
watching will donelley
in his silk shorts
& black irish hair

our dog shot between us
a white fury on tiny legs
not even a bark
straight for the jugular he went
the collie took off
tail between its legs
bloody hell said my sister
right i said
& stole a minute
to throw the daily mail
as fast as i could

hey up you two
a voice yelled from behind us
mr. marsh stood at his door
waving the daily
& pointing up the road
i suppose you'll
be taking some pups then
he said

we turned to see
our dog & the collie stuck
in that way of
love at first sight
bloody hell said my sister
right i said
& when dad asked how it went
my sister said
fine i think
& i said
we'll know in a few months
dad looked puzzled
& scratched his head
the dog just grinned & wagged

morning papers
*

my sister wanted a paper route
the motivator
prestige & cash
dad wasn't having it
too dangerous for a young lass

then one sunday
an absent paper boy &
the telegraphs & daily mails piled up

come on dad
i can do it she nagged
well all right said dad
but you're taking our kid
bugger i thought
& off we trudged

we got as far as marsh's farm
when trouble struck
furious barking
from a sheepdog
determined to round us up
same the next day & the next
on wednesday my sister said
we're taking the dog

we reached the top of the dirt road
up ahead the collie stretched
& ambled up the dirt
no rush
we were old news

cricket whites
*

you know how the light changes
when winter tucks itself back
under the cover of dark
& summer becomes
a prospect waiting
it was that kind of day
we packed cucumber sandwiches
a cork stoppered bottle
of dandelion & burdock
& caught the number fifty nine south
the remains of winter flashed
behind the haze of fogged windows
& i dreamed of cricket whites
muscular men clad in
slim ivory pants shirt sleeves rolled
& sturdy capable hands
polishing the dimpled curve
of a hard red ball
innocently unaware
that childish dreams had
relinquished their hold
& here i was on the edge of summer

turning the compost
*

dad unearthed a mouse nest
little pink babies with longish tails
i kept one in a shoe box even though
dad said it would die
i had hopes
& the long empty days of spring break
i tell you that shoe box was a wonder
if i could i would have shrunk
& lived in there with the mouse
just the two of us staring
at the postage stamp picture on the wall
counting stems of roses on
the crayoned wallpaper
& nestled in the comfort of dad's old sock
it died
dad cleared a space under the apple tree
dug a hole large enough for the shoe box &
i made a marker out of lollypop sticks & mum's nail polish
we covered him with rich dark earth & frayed apple blossom
planted the marker & a spray of dad's tea roses
i wept & dad said it's ok he's with his family now
but I knew he was not
they were still mourning
somewhere in the compost heap

we beat him fair & square
& tied him to the neighbor's fence
with his mother's torn up tea towel
& as we rode off into the sunset
my sister said
spacemen are stupid
i hope he's learned his lesson
nothing ever stops tonto & the ranger

later after the spanking from dad
& the no supper hunger pains kicked in
we sat on the bottom bunk
drawing pictures of pirates
& sylvia said
let's be pirates & buccaneers
& next time we see george wiggins
we'll make him walk the plank
tonto would never do that i say
she ponders for a moment then shrugs in agreement
yup she says neither would the ranger

we're captain blood & calico jack
we explained to our mother
ach kleines madchen she said
can't you play at something nicer
dad said
let 'em be it's character building
he arched a brow & looked over his pipe
but stay away from that wiggins boy
spacemen are trouble he said
we could make him walk the plank i said
he grins & says tonto would never do that
neither would the ranger
& slipped us a silver half crown each
dubloons we shriek ... arrrr he said

tonto & the ranger
*

sylvia was always the ranger
me the wild red indian
only because the hat & mask were hers
i had the bow & arrows
& slung from reedy childish hips
a silver colt six shooter
the same for her
& the broken handle from dad's garden spade
made a fine repeating rifle

we are the wild riders of the west
with a taciturn dream that good always wins
we whooped & hollered down boynton street
riding imaginary horses
until we were held at bay by george wiggins
in red gum boots
his mother's tea towel tied at the neck
& fluttering down his back it labeled him
a present from blackpool in faded gothic script

stop he yells
from behind his shiny ray gun
no indians allowed
come on our kid
my sister says
we'll ride down mansfield road instead
george sneers
you can't go down there either
that right there's planet jupiter
& it belongs to me

queen
*

i swim
i swim like a queen
like a queen with a tiara
that must never get wet
chin up
mouth dipping & sluicing
my arms like wings crushing the water
a small wave of anxiety trailing in my wake

this is how i learned to swim
grabbed neck & shoulders
monkey legs wrapped tight around my father
no dad i scream
but he unhooks me
throws me high & wide
& i am down below in blue & bubbles &
the sharp sting of water in my nose
i think
i will drown

hands haul me from the grip of fear
swing me to the white five by eight tiles of safety
you can swim he says

i nod & shiver from cold
then slide back into treachery
gripped fingers releasing one by one

you swim like a queen he says
i raise my head

i am a queen
queen of the mermaids
& i swim with a tiara on my head

rubber buttons
*

friday night was bath night in front of the kitchen fire
auntie clara boiling water on the stove
the steam making for
frizzled hair while
on the side a clothes horse huddled close to the fire
warming clean undies
knickers & cotton liberty bodices
rubber buttons all down the front
our little girl fingers could never quite
get the hang of squishing them through
double reinforced button holes
we'd stand damp & shivery
struggling to button up
once in a while a shank would give
& a button would fly like a bullet
we'd laugh &
dad would duck behind the newspaper
pipe clenched between his teeth then
he'd read the comic strips out loud
the gambols
an everyday country life featuring george & gayle
& our favorite
micky moran
who stood legs akimbo hands on hips
kimota he would shout
& in a flash he was transformed
marvelman in blue tights
we'd scream kimota at the top of our lungs
but nothing fixed those rubber buttons

rag n bone man
*

a pile of old sheets shirts & other stuff
set aside as used & done &
waiting to be tucked in to the jumble of his flat bed wagon
his sole companion was a well loved plug
who wore a hat with a faded red bandana
we'd hear his call over the clip of hooves
coming down the back alley
rag n bone
the first call sliding up an octave
rag n bo ... one
it sent us scurrying for sugar lumps
dad would meet us at the gate
a pile of old clothes under his arm
a pipe & tobacco in his pocket
we'd giggle at the horse's hairy snuffling
searching our outstretched palms for sugar lumps
dad would lean on the gate
& offer the rag n bone man a bowl of cavendish tobacco
they'd tamp their pipes & share the flame
from a match struck against
the sole of hob nail boots & then
they'd smoke in that companionable way
that pipe smokers seem to have
dad would tap the ashes from his pipe
& lift us up on the back of the cart
you can bring 'em back next week he'd joke
the rag n bone man would drive us down the street
& we'd scream rag n bo .. one
all the way there & back

obernkirchen
*

billowed feather beds bulging from open windows
catching sunlight & fresh air
oma's apartment
always with that potato onion kitchen smell &
the slight stink of fecal filled latrines coming up from the basement
we'd sleep in oma's bed
it was tall on legs of sturdy serviceable
that whispered of pine coned forests
& told secrets about our little known half brother
in oma's apartment we came to know that brother
half our mother's & half that belonged to his father
who was killed at the italian front
& never spoken of except cloistered among tut tutted war tales
the never enough rations & still unfound bombs
silently ticking the minutes & hours
until the perfect time to detonate arrived
flinging legs & arms skyward
a decapitated head or two rolling down the lane
avoiding the cart of milk churns waiting to be delivered
while we sat in the meadow grass
slurping frozen chocolate milk from the nice german milkman
& listened to horrors imagined or real
it was the best frozen milk ever
the best memory
oh & frank in his lederhosen

outside the starlings have returned
like leaves they gather
on the empty branches of winter
the orange cat tucks front legs in
& watches from behind brittle frozen fronds
i retrieve the scarf, place it round my neck
it smells of everything

the smell of everything
*

outside a skirl of starlings plague the yard
take off in startled pattern flight
& from behind the delicacy of brown tipped ferns
an orange cat emerges with casual strut & spring
to land upon the redwood fence
a seemingly easy balancing act

inside a body of empty clothes piled high
on the quilted counterpane
a heady tonic of pipe tobacco
revealed at every folding & unfolding
alongside the bed open boxes wait
to receive shirts & jackets, a plaid scarf
clothes that used to grace his shrinking frame
he wore that scarf like priestly vestment
i retrieve the scarf

a silver plated tray engraved with dust
occupies center stage on the glass covered dresser
it neatly holds his daily rituals
two briar pipes
brass coin dish
& a silver backed hairbrush still sheltering
strands of black & silver hair
to the left a trio of slim books leather bound
blake, keats, & a book of common prayer
his three reasons to start each day
in good humored expectation
all are placed inside a burl wood box
that still vaguely smells of pipe tobacco
i place the scarf on top

bakelite saints
*

plugged into the wall
saint joe & saint francis
glow saintly watchfulness
in the lower bunk
i push up feet into the sprung mattress above
hey our kid wake up
you mutter discontent into the pillowcase
can't sleep i whisper
them saints is keeping me up
unplug 'em you say & roll back into the pillow
i'm scared of the dark & things under the bed i say
you groan & slide off the bunk &
martyr them with sisterly justice
thanks i say
s' ok you say
& slide under the covers to give me a hug
we're church of england anyway

Ricocheted Memories

contents

bakelite saints	3
the smell of everything	4
obernkirchen	6
rag n bone man	7
rubber buttons	8
queen	9
tonto & the ranger	10
turning the compost	12
cricket whites	13
morning papers	14
will donelley	16
the dark horse	17
down town rain	20
roller skates	21
illuminations	22
the smell of men	24
home	25
gilding the words	26
purple spring	27
half pint	28
banshees & ghosts	29
two crowns	30
mum	31
the problem with sharing a bedroom	32
six miles of love	33
dance class	34
summer holidays	36
home	38
jefferson	39

Ricocheted Memories

poems by
Christina Quinn

www.ingramcontent.com/pod-product-compliance
Lightning Source LLC
Chambersburg PA
CBHW020634130526
44591CB00043BA/604